VANITAS

VANITAS

ANN DRYSDALE

Shoestring Press

All rights reserved. No part of this work covered by the copyright herein may be reproduced or used in any means – graphic, electronic, or mechanical, including copying, recording, taping, or information storage and retrieval systems – without written permission of the publisher.

Printed by imprintdigital
Upton Pyne, Exeter
www.digital.imprint.co.uk

Typesetting and cover design by narrator
www.narrator.me.uk
info@narrator.me.uk
033 022 300 39

Published by Shoestring Press
19 Devonshire Avenue, Beeston, Nottingham, NG9 1BS
(0115) 925 1827
www.shoestringpress.co.uk

First published 2019
© Copyright: Ann Drysdale
© Cover image: "Ready for the Snow" by George Lucas.
Reproduced by permission of the artist.
© Author photograph by Derek Adams

The moral right of the author has been asserted.

ISBN 978-1-912524-29-7

ACKNOWLEDGEMENTS

Thanks are due to the editors of journals in which some of these poems first appeared. They include Acumen, Prole, Zoomorphic Magazine, The New Statesman, The Chimaera, The Oldie, The Spectator, Now Culture, and The Flea.

For the ghosts between the pages.
Thank you for your company.

CONTENTS

Upon First Looking into a Gideon Bible.	1
Lost Boy	2
Way to Go… *Alabaster and Obsidian*	3
My Father Practises Penmanship	4
Her Berry	5
Kintsugi	6
Road	7
Under	8
Vision in Winter	9
From the Diary of the Queen of Naples	10
Moist	11
Just Desserts	12
Queen of Cups	13
Room On Top	14
Mea Culpa	15
Small Rodents, Dead	16
God's Island	17
Way to Go… *The Lyke Wake Talk*	18
It's a Snip	20
Shearing Day	21

Baa	22
Heads and Helves	23
Dog Days	24
The It of Me	
Oooh! Aaah! Dog Guitar!	
Winterreise	
Saint Luke's Little Summer	
Old-dog Easy	
Doggone	
Assistant Wanted	28
Kikuchiyo	29
A Sea View	30
Neighbourhood Watch	31
A Long Legged Fly	32
Dung Beetle	33
Sewerage Emergency	34
Way to Go…	35
"Edward"	
Too Much Sky	36
Bald Patches	37
Against Satire	38
Strictly Private	39
Do I feel lucky?	40
Ballade des Odeurs du Temps Jadis	42
Ben Gunn Weeps	43
A Passing Phase	44

Connie Calls   45
: *Ripping the Knitting*
: *Picking through Wrack*
: *Staying on Top*
: *Urn*

She Forgets to Phone   48

When I have fears…   49

Solstice   50

I Think Not   51

Sparrowfart   52

Way to Go…   53
: *Carriage Return*

UPON FIRST LOOKING INTO A GIDEON BIBLE.

I, too, am in Arcadia, says the book.
You measure out your lives in rented rooms,
assume I'm there, although you never look.
I am the voice of your collective dooms.
I'm an unwanted promise, a poor thing
with no desire to educate or please.
Handle me, and my arbitrary string
cuts you a slice of text, like so much cheese.
I watch you go, as all have gone before,
lurching from accident to consequence.
I am the small reminder in the drawer
that you are simply a coincidence.
I am a constant, a sad paradigm
for shrinking distance and compressing time.

LOST BOY

Not long after your picture had been filed
the press began to circulate another.
Your brief appearance as "drowned Syrian child"
was superseded by your little brother.

The media reviewed the human damage
and Don McCullin with his Magnum eye
explained why Aylan's was the single image
your tragedy will be remembered by.

You were too clearly dead; he seemed asleep.
He was the Twitter *"Ooh"*, the Facebook *"Aww"*.
His was the picture that they chose to keep;
an easy icon for a distant war.

Your likeness now is difficult to find.
Not quite so cute, and yet a lot more true,
uncomfortable, best put out of mind.
This poem, Ghalib Kurdi, is for you.

WAY TO GO...

Alabaster and Obsidian

When I was little, all my life ago,
I learned the secrets of the haruspex,
making projections for my adult life
by studying the guts of Pelicans.

There I uncovered archaeology.
Wandered in black and white across Sumeria,
borne in the lion-sledge of Queen Shub-Ad,
learning the new language of found things.

Words that constructed their own definitions
for want of scholarship to pin them down;
Kassite and Kuri-galzu, Ziggurat
and Alabaster and Obsidian.

The last two were the ones I got to keep,
the special pebbles that stayed in my pocket
when many others had been dropped and lost
or chucked back into the encroaching sea.

All that is left of the lost masterplan,
I slip them now and then into my mouth,
spit them, wet, into the palm of my hand
to see if I can still find their old shine.

I always do. So, ready the Ur-sledge
to haul my carcase into the hereafter
in an alabaster sarcophagus
with obsidian knobs.

MY FATHER PRACTISES PENMANSHIP

There in the buff-coloured exercise book
the wise words stayed unfaded as the years
strode firmly forward, leaving them behind.
Every so often I would ask my Gran
if I could have another look at them
and she would fetch the book and find the page
to show me "that's what Jimmy did at school".
Two sentences, written again-again
on facing pages. I would whisper them,
two truths that I would stitch into the lining
of my expanding head. These things are so.
The apple has ten brown seeds.

I gradually came to understand
that nowadays it isn't always thus.
Sometimes there's short change in the chewy pockets;
modifications mean deficiencies.
I cannot now believe in what he knew
nor take on trust the innards of an apple.
All that is left me is the facing page
whereon the little boy whose ten brown seeds
were his honest testament to forever
wrote something else, again, again, again
that has survived him into the future.
The carrot is the root of the plant.

HER BERRY

Always a berry, never a *beret*,
my grandmother was seldom seen without it.
Long use had trained it to observe its purpose,
holding her round head in a woollen bowl
warming the precious thoughts she handed out
one at a time, like pocket-soft boiled sweets,
to the small girl who guzzled them and grew.

There was another one she kept for best,
funerals, weddings and "when comp'ny come".
It still maintained the nap, the naughty nipple,
the crease that indicated its circumference.
She wore it warily, tucking it back
into the whiffy tissue in the moth-drawer,
muttering "silly thing looks like a cowpat".

After she died, taking the berry with her,
I kept the cowpat, undertook its training
in how to hold a head and keep it happy.
It has begun to relish an adventure,
slowly relaxing into readiness
to share the grubby garden things she showed me,
out in the rain she taught me not to fear.
It's not a berry yet but, with her help,
I'm working on it.

KINTSUGI

The art of precious mending

Gran was an artist when it came to mending.
She looked on darning as an act of kindness
and introduced me to the theory,
thrusting a wooden mushroom up a sock.

Mending is not like making; any knots
or loose ends must end up on the outside.
The sock wears at the point where the shoe rubs;
the hole is there to show you where it hurts.

Take a blunt needle with an easy eye
and a long ringlet of unravelled knitting.
The colour doesn't matter. Choose soft wool
to weave a little cushion for the ouch.

Weasel it in and out and up and under
while you imagine somebody you love
pulling that sock over a poorly foot
to feel your darn kissing the sore place better.

ROAD

Give me a low road slicing across a fen
with stiff reeds wuthering in a steady wind.
Or else a wet grey ribbon of tarmacadam
stretched out from here to wherever, dawdling
under a bowl of sky

Show me a straight road between crinkled walls
rolling through rodings at a thoughtful pace
shoulder to shoulder with a listless river,
ignoring it until they kiss and part
under a stone bridge.

I am drowning aloud in too many mountains.
Find me a flat pink road, rolled out like carpet
with high wires moaning along the length of it,
a road that goes the distance between square towers
under a threat of rain.

UNDER

Out, oh, out under the bumbershoot.
All drops diverted to the lower thirds
of trouserlegs that scissor freezing air
making wet slap and to the ankles clinging.

Or out without, taking the full-on hammering
of the waterpins through the apparel,
barrelling onto the bowed head
of the scurrying old skin-soaker.

Better the latter; lovelier over.
Then in, spinaround, keyturn and kettle,
welcoming, singing out in a warm waft,
giving the lie to the inclement memory.

A wet coat makes a hanged man on the door
drips like a stalactite, one, two, three, four
into the boots beneath it on the floor.

VISION IN WINTER

In Yoknapatawpha County we made love
and became all in all to one another.
It was a literary thing, a shared obsession.
I read the novels in a needy rush
so as to join him in the fantasy.
Working in secret, I contrived a gift
to celebrate that fine *folie à deux*.

Night after night, knees wrapped in scarlet flannel
I sewed white satin ribbon criss and cross
and overlaid it with a slimmer blue.
I scissored out the necessary stars
and fixed them with my needle into place,
drawing my own blood with each poke and pick,
each stitch-stitch-stitch of adolescent love.

We left behind our Sound and Fury days
to carve new paths in different disciplines.
A lifetime later, growing overtones
have made that flag an object of disgust
but when I ask around from time to time
to find out how he's doing, I recall
the look I once put on his face with it
and with the fumbled loving long ago
in London, under less contentious stars.

FROM THE DIARY OF THE QUEEN OF NAPLES

Most days, and every night, I think of him.
The lover I betrayed and left behind.
When I was very small, he was my brother
But as I grew I learned to think of him
In ways that were no longer innocent.
I lied to Father, said I went to him
To help him with his literacy skills
But when we were alone, oh, how we played!
I loved his face and never thought him ugly
I loved his body in a hundred ways,
Each one a glorious experiment.
At first he hurt me with his clumsiness
But kissed me when I cried. He made me laugh.
He cut his fingernails at my behest
And touched me where I told him.
I lived for our encounters. I dare swear
That Father was completely in the dark
Till an unguarded whisper broke our spell
And stirred up an unprecedented storm.
I was afraid. I said he tried to rape me.
I lied and his love did not contradict me.
Instead he took the words that I had taught him
And used his tongue to cut his precious throat.
So when the strangers came and I, amazed
By Father's crafty silvering of mirrors,
Was duped into that monumental promise,
I threw away the chance to put it right.
I wonder where he is and how he fares.
I long for him. I walk alone at night
Telling the truth to the indifferent moon:
I gave my heart but Father gave my hand
And now I live a lie with Ferdinand.

MOIST

How is your liver? Good? I have to say
my salmon is particularly moist.

I can recall the shiver of disgust
as I attempted to unhear the word.
Not *salmon*, the fine leaping silver fish
or the pink flesh of it, soft on the plate
of the man I have lately come to love,
but the emetic adjective, m-*euch*,
I cannot bear to have in my mouth.
I want to stuff it back into your face
via the prissy *moue* through which it issued,
the momentary artificial sphincter
not called-for by the word's pronunciation,
the little *tup-tup* lipsmack it implied.

The candle gutters in the smoky jar
making familiar sequins in your eyes.
Sharing a wine-smile and an understanding
we push our chairs back, rise and move away,
that word forgiven and almost forgotten.
Please leave it lying on the dining table;
let us not take it up into the bedroom,
a word that cannot ever have to do with
the gentle sweat of our proposed encounter,
slippery mysteries of lubrication,
the shared saliva of a lovers' kiss.

JUST DESSERTS

The weighted plate sits in the chipped dish
hunkering down onto the summer pudding
so as to kettle the unruly fruit
as it bleeds out into the greedy crust.

Gradually the identities mingle.
The crimson currant merges with the white,
skins slip aside and pippy innards seep
into the soft cushions of the raspberries.

When all is sodden I will conjure up
old ghosts to share my feast. See how they blend –
he who called all my cooking "dripping rubbish",
he who "yes-butted" and knew better methods,
he who feared seeds under his dental plate;
sit down, the lot of you, and watch me eat.

QUEEN OF CUPS

She was my senior by several years.
I lusted after her, the way girls do
while they are sorting through their new hormones.

I have that photograph of the school trip
when she, as prefect, supervised our bathing,
leading us, wet and laughing, up the beach
to our piled clothes and towels. There she is,
leaning into the slope, her perfect breasts
two matching eggs above the waiting cups
of the slipped top of her grown-up swimsuit.

The hormones fell into place like cast dice.
Heterosexuality prevailed
but we were friends until she went away.
I filed her memory; the Queen of Cups,
spilling herself in that old photograph.

They told me she was back. Treatment for cancer.
I asked her round to talk about old times,
steeling myself to handle any change
in her appearance. I swear there was none.

I bought cake. I remembered she loved cake.
And coffee. As I raised the pot to pour
she made as if to stop me. Then she smiled.
I have to watch the caffeine nowadays –
just the one cup and I, despite myself,
stole a swift glance and wondered – just the one?

ROOM ON TOP

When I was young I knew my boobs were far
from perfect, so I coaxed them to the norm
with ends of a baguette, stuffed in a bra
that revelled in the name of Maidenform.

As time went by, they ceased to seem inferior;
they grew, they pulled, they firmed and filled and fed.
They ticked the box in each of the criteria
for boobs, without resort to bits of bread.

And then the lump, the panic and the knife.
The simple common sense of giving up
a pound or so of flesh to keep a life.
A broken jug swapped for an empty cup.

So once again I turn to kitchen gimmicks
to counteract a unilateral sag.
A miracle of silicone that mimics
a chicken fillet in a plastic bag.

MEA CULPA

I broke the silence, right? All by myself.
I took it, a bit at a time, and murdered it.
The early morning fart, the creaking fidget,
mumbled encouragement of puzzled dog.
Grunting of bending to sensible shoes
and *phew* at the achievement of the knot.
Squeak open and click shut. Toenails on tarmac.
Sixfooted shuffle on the way through the woods.
Ha! – as the white chest of the watching cat
shrank to a tuft of sheepswool on a thorn.
The first *G'morning* shattered the last crust
and then I handed over to the wren
who took the wreck and made a song of it.

SMALL RODENTS, DEAD

Each death is different. A murdered vole
lies in a frozen dive, its stiffened legs
stretched fore-and-aft in a flat capriole.

A rat seems only sleeping, soft and slack;
there is no malice in it any more,
a brief apology might bring it back.

Two shrews lie face-to-face, their fists clenched tight,
frozen forever in a punch-up pose
as though not going down without a fight.

A broken mouse, with its one teacup ear
still spread to catch the warning that it missed
and half-ball eye still shimmering with fear.

Felis domesticus has done its worst;
which fallen hero shall I bury first?

GOD'S ISLAND

O my children, now thou art surely blessed.
It being Christmas or somebody's birthday,
there is within thy reach new Plasticine.

Peel thou the pale skin from the flaccid fruit
and savour the aroma of its flesh
as you revere it with your little hands.

From chalk and Vaseline and fatty acid
I have made these fine strips of perfect colour.
Now you must make the sacrifice of praise.

Make me an island, using every piece,
keeping the colours separate and true,
a fine mosaic of sweet, soft tesserae.

Oh, nip and squeeze and press the virgin dough,
make trees and flowers and strange animals.
Leave but the whiff of it upon your fingers.

Offer it up!
        Then trample and destroy,
crush and annihilate, murder the colours,
mash them to greasy anonymity.

You have pleased me. This is my gift to you;
A warm ball of vanilla possibility.
Take it my children. Go forth and create!

WAY TO GO…

The Lyke Wake Talk

> *This ae neet, this ae neet,*
> *Ivvery neet and all,*
> *Fire an' fleet an' candleleet,*
> *And Christ receive thy saul.*
> – The Lyke-wake Dirge. Trad. Yorks

Old neighbours will gather to carry me
Over the moor to Osmotherley
Setting me down intermittently
To hide from the wind and remember me.

> *Just this once, just this once*
> *Now and again and often*
> *They'll wheel me out to talk about*
> *And never mind the coffin*

At Low Cote they'll think of the pony
That shied at the shushing of air brakes
To scatter the spuds from his panniers
And take off the tip of my finger.

> *Just this once, just this once*
> *Now and again and often*
> *They'll wheel me out to talk about*
> *And never mind the coffin*

At Arnsgill they'll mention the morning
I flung my coat over my shoulder
And set off a cordon of beaters
While the guns were halfway to the butts.

> *Just this once, just this once*
> *Now and again and often*
> *They'll wheel me out to talk about*
> *And never mind the coffin*

At Birkwood they'll talk of the clipping
When I sweated as catcher and wrapper
And then, when the jenny went funny
I handsheared two ewes while they fixed it.

> *Just this once, just this once*
> *Now and again and often*
> *They'll wheel me out to talk about*
> *And never mind the coffin*

And on Douglas Rigg they'll remember
The day we all gathered the Common,
When three thousand sheep ran before us
And thirty of them were mine…

IT'S A SNIP

Ball Brothers, Ball Brothers, Burgon and Ball
Show me the shiniest sheep-shears of all.
I am no mere shearer, I am a gun.
Gaspers and riggwelters? Mate, bring 'em on!
I shi-ack the drummer and tell him to stick
To wigging and dagging and ringing his dick.
I pink the whole tally from cobbler to catch
For I am the ringer that no-one can match.
Ball Brothers, Ball Brothers, Burgon and Ball
Show me the shiniest sheep-shears of all.

SHEARING DAY

In a check shirt, buttoned-up boyswise
but not right to the top. Perilous, possible.
Head bent over the tossed fleece, kneeling
and reaching to the rolling; stink of sheep
shot through with the whiff of her own armpits,
joyfully conscious of the breasts between.

Borrowed jeans, dodgy fly, property of a brother,
loose and sliding over the hip as she straightens,
pulling the neckwool in random handfuls toward her,
twisting and teasing it into a greasy rope,
leaning to tie the bundle tight, then rising,
stretching up high to chuck it into the sheet.

That action admits to the presence of simple knickers
but hints at the absence of anything under the shirt.
She hitches the jeans, lifting a leg can-can high
to step over the rail into the catching-pen,
choose a fit ewe to drag out onto the floor,
upend and offer to the nearest shearer.

Offering, too, the new thing she has discovered
here in the shearing shed. Proud, pulling her weight,
showing her skill, surprising herself with her stamina,
shimmering gleefully in and out of her element.
She is man, among men, doing a man's work
but, oh, she is woman now as never before.

BAA

It was the plaintive cry that summoned me,
connecting to the shepherd in my head,
telling me that somebody needed help.

She had been fighting to escape the wire
that held her fast. Now she had given up,
settled for waiting and the random cry.

I pulled her free and hauled her to her feet.
She ran off, shouting Baa! and two fine lambs
stepped into view and scuttled in to suck.

Job done. She wandered off, leaving her thanks
in the form of a fresh tuft of wool
that came away easily in my hand.

The weather's warm, her fleece was well-risen
with a smear of soft yolk on the skin side.
She'll make sweet shearing for some lucky soul.

The wool is with me now, a fuzzy rose
smelling of precious flesh, reminding me
that the old shepherd in me searches still.

HEADS AND HELVES

Over the years these heads have fallen off
but they can still speak, muttering their stories
to who-will-listen.
And who will listen? One who witnessed it
and who remembers when a ringing thud
turned to a clack.
A hollow clack as evening-weary arms
allowed one head to miss the waiting stake
and broke its neck.
A broken wooden neck, one among many
forsaken bits of ash and hickory
that once held heads.
That once held heads as did the fleshy necks
of human heads whose severance depended
on others' skills.
Those other skills that skulls depended on
for tidy sundering. Cromwell, Mishima
The Queen of Scots.
Poor Queen of Scots, poor Tom, poor Yukio,
who took the hacking of rank amateurs
before the end.
Before the end afforded by the loss
of ruined heads. But these heads are all whole,
lost at a stroke.
Lost at a stroke, they lie, a rusting pile
of various business ends I have contrived
to sever clean.
So, severed clean, sledge-hammer, maul and mattock,
they can be fixed. Meanwhile I give them names
of heads less lucky.

DOG DAYS

The It of Me

Oh, it love me. It say it love me.
Me make wanting and it perform,
always.

It there, me sleeping.
Not long me waking up and out.
It bootsfirst but not long, me needful.

Door in-and-out and dark street waiting.
It bump one-two, me clickit three-four-five.
It busy head, me busy messages.

Me doggish fossicking, it no patience sometimes.
Ow! Pull my neck!
I trick it then – sit and look why? Then it go funnyface,
Say sorry-sorry and do happyhands.

In big grass and high trees, me go nolead,
but not free, for it once-ago name me. Name bind stronglead.
Me far and it loudname. Me come thunder, grinning with teeth.
It give small edible and happyhands.

Aaaah! Happyhands! Only on head outdoors, but in,
in, go everywhere, all the pits of my limbs and Oh,
feely, feely into my belly. It sniff my feet.
It make love.

Me please it easily. A look, a lick,
rough buggeroff for sudden stranger,
make it do often food and happyhands.

Oooh! Aaah! Dog Guitar!

Lift me up like you did when I was small
Hold me, enfold me, don't let me fall
I'll lean on your bosom and I'll flash my teeth
If you pick with your fingers on my underneath
Oh, love me true and love me tender
Make me quiver like a furry Fender
Rock me and roll me, give me wings
Strum on my tum till my tight skin sings
Don't waste on air what you can play on me
The touch-me tango – ecstasy

Winterreise

One fine day on the brittle rim of winter
Hoarfrost crisp on the whiskers of the grasses
One old woman galumphing down a mountain
One small dog with a definite advantage
Four legs good and two manifestly less so
Slip-slide-skittering as the scree unfreezes
"Damn these knees, they're no longer fit for purpose
Hang on, Dogface – don't go too far without me!"
Not an order so much as a suggestion
But he waits, sitting primly in the sunshine
Falls in biddably as she overtakes him
Trims his step to her elderly progression
As they cover the final stage together
He is thinking it might be worth a biscuit

Saint Luke's Little Summer

He is here at Fishguard again, biting the water
as it comes out under the bridge and into the sea.
Telling it straight and loudly, giving it what-for,
up to his oxters among the scurrying bubbles
nipping and yapping with self-important joy.

Canine Canute, the river never obeys him
but year after year he's gone down to the meeting of waters
playing the game till he tires and comes to heel
rubbing his dogface up and down my leg
in a sweet semblance of friendship, drying his whiskers.

This time I wondered if he'd be up to the journey
but as soon as he knew that he was in sniffing distance
he tensed like a gundog that knows when its work is waiting,
sat still to be freed of his lead, then set off yelping
like a furry fool to the place where he needed to be.

By the waters of Abergwaun, there I sat down.
Yea, I wept as I watched an old dog doing his duty
plodging as ever among the chattering pebbles
his hoarse voice crossly admonishing the river
as it ran regardless over his paws to the sea.

Old-dog Easy

We have come at last to an accommodation.
Stopping in the negotiated places
where the lead goes on and the treat goes in
with no more need for a formal command.
That's just as well, you having grown deaf
and me not always quick to find the whistle.

Using your rediscovered puppy-strut
you make a daily joy of your new leg
but when the squirrel froze for a moment,
a perfect target on the road ahead,
you stiffened, then relaxed and let it go –
Nah – life's too short. I know, old dog, I know.

Doggone

Oh, he is dead now, the little scruffy dog
with the extraordinary eyebrows. He's gone,
taking his gaiety and his fine friendship.

Passer-by, peering sideways through the window
can you see the sorrow in the quiet house,
snapshot of a world in the process of change?

Bed tipped up, waiting to be put out of sight
along with the cushion that still whiffs of him.
Future heartaches tucked under the furniture.

Plate on the floor, gravy congealing unlicked,
promise kept in a second of forgetting.
Leads coiled like mooring-ropes when a boat has sailed.

Old cat expanding to fit the sudden space.
Slippered ballerina cocking a stiff leg
over a gone gate at the foot of the stairs.

ASSISTANT WANTED

Must be able to work on own initiative.
To read what I write and tell me what I'm saying.
To hear what I say and write it without asking.

To munch steadily and in some sort of order
through all the accumulated paper promises
and clear a small space in the centre for possibility.

To push a birch broom at the gathering of slurry
encroaching over the edges of my surfaces
so as to conjure a ribbon of light through the middle.

To dive on a signal at a moment's notice
and take with a perfectly timed one-handed catch
the dull *whup* of a well-aimed lump of caring.

To spirit away all living liabilities
and dance with them for as long as may seem necessary
under the half-closed eye of an occasional moon.

KIKUCHIYO

Having you makes me happy. Just a few
crumbs of the stinky kibble in the pond
and you will rise to the occasion. You
will rocket to the surface and beyond,
landing on lilies with a bare-arse slap
(fishmonger whacking cod on greaseproof paper)
and then the victory roll, the farewell flap
of your flat tail, the final caudal caper
as you slip between leaves and disappear.
My fat-lipped gentleman, my slippery boy,
my pleasure dangles on the edge of fear.
My funny, finny, feisty, ghosty koi,
heron and heatwave haunt the boundary
where love becomes responsibility.

A SEA VIEW

There are crisp legs spread all over the balcony
pink and white, artless and opened up to the sky.
Detached and ownerless, posing perpetual questions:
Whose bones? Whose charnel house? Whose wasted crusts?

The white bird tumbles clumsily out of the sun
carrying a small crab like a novelty reticule
held ostentatiously in its tight tweezer-beak,
every leg pedalling, each one on its unicycle,
all giving it get-away with nowhere to go.

The bird lands, looks at me, arch, inscrutable,
casting the crab onto the littered bitumen
then tossing it onto its back and making a meal of it
with a single jack-hammer blow to its savoury guts.

With a flutter of feathery napery over the table
it takes French leave of the dregs of its quivering breakfast,
upending the carapace like an empty eggshell,
leaving the bony soldiers to die in the sun.

NEIGHBOURHOOD WATCH

Jack is moving in under the eaves
of number twelve. It's a new-build development;
he made the hole himself. It's still quite small.
His wife peers anxiously out of its roundness,
her small black head perched on her silver ruff,
a truffle on a salver. Here comes Jack
with a nice stick. Too bad it's far too big.
He pokes it crossways, this way and now that
then lets it fall. It settles on the pile
of failed attempts that gather at my feet.
Then off he goes to get another one.
Catching his wife's inscrutable blue eye
I raise a thumb and wink, miming a promise –
leave it to me, OK?

Quickly I gather up all Jack's big sticks,
wave at his wife, break them across my knee
into a lot of lesser sticks and scatter them
around the place that he collects them from.
Next time he comes he brings a stick that fits
and his wife turns it into furniture.

I'm not a bad old bird, as neighbours go.
As Jack would tell you, if he only knew.

A LONG LEGGED FLY

There was no stream and the thing wasn't moving.
In the cat's water-dish it lay, a pulled thread
tweaked summarily from the seam of a cheap top,
twiddled absentmindedly between finger and thumb
and flicked like a bogey into oblivion.

No more than a few floating whiskers, perceptibly dead,
nothing left to connect it to its former identity.
A fly once, probably, spoiling the fresh surface.
Out of the waste paper basket I whisked an old tissue
to dab it off, like a smut from a toddler's cheek.

Before finally folding its shroud to squish and bin it
I took a quick look at the blob of sodden insectitude
seeing it stir, feeling a quiet excitement
as the soft cushion sucked off the dripping coating
that was binding it damply to its impending end.

It reached out each one of its thin six into a tiptoe
taking its weight as it found two sycamore wings
then, feet close together, stretched into itself like a cat.
I held it for twelve in-and-outs of slowed, shallow breathing
till it took off into the blustery afternoon.

DUNG BEETLE

Here he comes, dribbling singlemindedly,
concentrating, keeping control of the ball.
And there he goes down the wing,
the wing actual, the wing ephemeral,
beating half-hearted defenders who don't really go for it.
Nobody wants possession of his ball
only the cheap thrill of the actual tackle,
the nom-nom nourishment stuffed up his shiny shirt.
See, off he goes, on he goes, while the ball swells and slows,
gathering unto itself the shit of its conception
the aim of its only begetter
as he dribbles, dribbles, heading head-down for the line.
And he scores!

SEWERAGE EMERGENCY

*A regular occurrence hereabouts
in times of heavy rainfall.*

O fons spurcatus! Fifty shades of brown!
Thou flowest by the footpath into town
With tails of tampons and with skins of towels
And, tissue-wrapped, the gifts of human bowels.

With every sudden flood, the geyser blows
And all around its shameful shower it throws,
Denying passers-by the choice to question
The truths of menstruation and digestion.

As if he would convince me that the scene
Was not as nasty as it might have been,
All unaware of his own irony,
A blackbird (genus *Turdus*) sang to me.

Biodegradability, he cried
Is nature's answer to the nut-brown tide
And soon, with reek and rot and gentle rain,
Only the stationery will remain.

WAY TO GO...

"Edward"

My old boat will come back for me at the end.
The bitter stink of the coal-dust in its bilges
will carry the lost past like the sly cologne
of a long-ago lover.

Broken or sunken for so long, he will find it,
wring the black water out of its sodden timbers
and come for me with it, showing the stamp still wet
on his Skipper's ticket.

We will lie, Charon and I, on the roof of the cabin,
the tops of our heads hard against one another,
hands round each other's wrists holding the process
in a safe grip.

We will breathe, while our busy legs pedal together,
hobnails conjuring sparks from invisible brickwork,
legging our way through the echoing green-grown darkness
of the final tunnel.

TOO MUCH SKY

July 1944

That was the day when there was too much sky.
Nobody came to get her out of bed
and when she went by herself to the window
yesterday's everything had disappeared.

Everybody was busy and shouting
and when at last the feet came on the stairs
something inside insisted she should run
across the room and jump back into bed.

Someone came in and sat down quietly
and said the little boy across the road
wouldn't be coming over for a while.
He and his Mum had had to go away.

He wanted her, they said, to have Blue Bear
to keep for him. But Blue Bear had got wet
although it wasn't raining and he smelt
of the fireplace first thing in the morning.

Alone again, she went back to the window.
How odd of Raymond, when he went away,
to take his house with him but leave Blue Bear.
She didn't like that there was too much sky.

BALD PATCHES

July 2017

I'm here as usual, in the place we shared.
Not much has changed, although a darker carpet
came in response to the red wine you spilled.

I watched a bit of Wimbledon without you.
Young Andy Murray's made the second round,
his bald spot growing with each interview.
John McEnroe now wears a pale yarmulke
over the memory of unruly curls.

Now in the bed we shared I lie alone
with the old dog rip-snoring at my feet.
I turn towards the rough wall on my right;
the fig tree is still there outside the window.

I turn, lie supine, breathe and turn again.
There on my left, as ever, lies your ghost,
hunched in the still-familiar position.
I've let it age with me so I won't lose it.
Pursing my lips I blow the fine white hair
that strives to hide the vulnerable scalp
making a place to plant a phantom kiss.

AGAINST SATIRE

A Faustian farewell to the New Statesman Competition

Settle thy studies, Annie, and begin;
Summon thy petty wit, thy will to win.
A Staggers comp? What doctrine call you this?
To take the Bung, the Mickey and the Piss.
To bob up grinning in a jingly hat
Waving a bladder. What's the point of that?
Why should I join a gang who merely sneer
At what a scholar should have learned to fear.
Elected worthies who, in office, choose
To whoop like idiots at PMQs
Or clever men who posit revolutions
That lead to punchlines rather than solutions.
Or sleek young men who fight with quip and pun
To win a pittance, take a bow and run.
Go, plan that insurrection in thy bar
No, I'll not enter. *Che sera, sera.*
A world hell-bound in handcart-mounted rush
Howls for a dragshoe, not a sodding push.
Get thee behind me, Satire. Thou shalt pass
To truth I'll bow, and thou can'st kiss mine Arse.

STRICTLY PRIVATE

I dream of whizzing in Vienna's waltzes,
a weightless penguin-driven shuttlecock;
of tangos intimate as peristalsis
belly-to-belly in a languid lock
with a flat-hatted Buenos Airean.
Or booty-bobbing to a reggae beat
with an accommodating Rastafarian.
Sometimes I jive on little twinkling feet,
whisking my knickers through my partner's crotch
and yet the intermittent passing Tom,
compelled to peep, will only get to watch
a taste of aspiration, gathered from
my solo un-coordinated bop
around the kitchen with a squidgy mop.

DO I FEEL LUCKY?

I came across a slow-worm in a wood.
I saw it clearly but a little late,
making me stumble suddenly aside
so that I wouldn't put a foot on it.

The dog peered at it, but with little more
than passing interest in a fellow-creature.
I picked it up to move it off the path,
thrilled by the feel of it, smooth in my hand.

I took delight in the blunt head of it
pushing between my fingers; the dry slide
as it dripped from the safety of my grasp
and took possession of the ground I gave it.

I put leaves over it; it thrust its head
up into daylight from a space between them.
I blessed it with a single fingertip
and it ducked down and drizzled out of sight.

That was a lucky day for pseudo-snakes.
What if a different poet had been there?
One with a good aim and a log to hand
might have made short work of its loveliness.

A different woman with a different dog,
a squealer with a killer, might have put
a noisy and uncomfortable stop
to its uncomplicated innocence.

It seems the end of everything depends
upon which agent of apocalypse
steps from the shadows when the chips are down.
Saviour or slaughterer. Call heads or tails.

I will spend no more time on hedging bets.
Bring on the Rapture when the time is right.
I'll take my chances, knowing as I do
the arbitrary nature of salvation.

BALLADE DES ODEURS DU TEMPS JADIS

Tell me, where is the air of Mum
 (Deodorant, that is, not mother)
The Johnson's pong of baby-bum
The fruity Brut of younger brother
The gay bouquet of Aunty May
Whose Coty kiss I used to fear
 Each time she came or went away –
Where are the whiffs of yesteryear?

The memories are sweet and vague
 Evening in Paris, Aqua Manda
Old posies clutched against the plague
 Each one a potent nose-pomander
In armpit, cleavage, lady-garden
 Back of neck and knee and ear
The human hum to hide and pardon –
Where are the whiffs of yesteryear?

BEN GUNN WEEPS

"Tell me, shipmates, do you perchance have cheese
aboard this vessel?" When they said they did
he wept a little, and when he was asked
to name his favourite, whispered "Wensleydale".
And then he dreamed again; this time with hope.

Now he could see the cheese, wrapped in its muslin,
close-crafted by a time-served artisan.
Perhaps a little mould, as they unwrapped it,
would fall like green tears on the wooden board.
Oh, knife or wire? How would they cut his piece;
his piece of eight, his piece of Wensleydale?

He saw it falling painlessly away
from the white, crumbling side of a soft cliff.
He tasted it, one salty nutty lump
at a slow, timeless time. His fingers dabbed
at its imaginary crumbs, anticipating.

But while he was away in Paradise,
the world had turned to show a sadder side.
The predatory short term interest
of the financial sector had changed cheese
making it caper to a new hornpipe;
short shelf-life and capricious innovation,
all the cut corners of the swift turnover,
the quest for the discretionary buck.

They brought a pallid slab, shrink-wrapped in plastic,
sleek and damp and beshitten with cranberries.
His toothless mouth rounded into a howl
and he wept with the grief of his great loss.

A PASSING PHASE

Out of the dark a sharp sliver,
there if you know where to look.
French manicured tip just clearing
the curved end of a dark finger.

Feeding on the dead day, growing
quick and strong into a bright stripe,
sharp centre of the cold eye
of an invisible goat.

Straight back, swollen belly,
strong, fecund and filled with possibility.
Feeling that it should stop while it's winning.
Knowing that it can only grow.

Breasts full and bottom blooming;
midlife midwife, all ways beaming,
planting the thought that this time could be different,
that it could go either way.

Turnaround. Flat chest and sunken belly,
back curved into a permanent shrug.
Pressed forward by a dowager's hump,
leaning into the inevitable.

At last a husk merely,
so nearly not there that it is irrelevant.
No group gathered with thanks or applause,
nothing much to remember

Easing backwards out of the door,
holding it open till the last moment
with the curved end of a dark toe,
a small bright nail only just proud of it.

CONNIE CALLS

Ripping the Knitting

Here we go on a circular needle, Fair Isle,
no back-and-forth, no row-end change of grip.
Every row plain, all loops thrown over backward,
each pattern on a regular repeat.

Almost a daily doddle, recognising
familiar images as they come round;
fir tree, snowflake, funny little triangle,
dealing with each on easy autopilot.

Knitting my way through daily conversations,
shamefully ticking off each group of stitches,
making the moves that regulate the tension,
saying the words that keep the pattern right.

But every now and then the yarns get tangled,
reminding me the thing's diminishing.
Now and again I must knit two together,
losing the plot a snowflake at a time.

This garment is for you, each clicking stint
is deftly tailored to your changing person
but still I wish that I could blitz the knitting,
ripping it back to where it last made sense.

Picking through Wrack

The phone is back once more against my ear.
We have performed the given ritual:
"Guess who!" "Oh, I dunno. The Queen of Sheba?"
It starts with laughter but it always slides
towards a door that swings on well-oiled hinges
to open onto a well-trodden pathway.
We walk again on the deserted beach

where you take me now more and more often,
the once-familiar changing day by day
in small uncertain steps that match your own.

The going's slippery underfoot.
My hand is ready under your elbow
to catch you when you stray, and if you fall.
Here and there in the seaweed are small things
catching the light. Wet pebbles, chips of glass
that hold their colour, are still what they were.

I wander head down, picking these small treasures
carefully out of all that salty wrack
holding them up to show you how they shine
before I tuck them into your coat pocket
hoping to help them stay a little longer
above the level of the rising tide.

Staying on Top

Today we are skipping like bugs on custard
but still the phone hangs heavy in my hand.
Your great-grandchildren have been visiting
and you are giving me the gist of it.

"They were so sweet I could have eaten them!"
I run to meet you over the shiny surface;
here is a happiness that I can hold for you:
"Tell me about them, love. What are their names?"

Too sharp a question, piercing the thin skin,
opens a hole into the cold coagulation
lying in wait under the bright moments.
A quick step backward, flicking a wet foot,
"it doesn't matter; it'll come back later".
I try too hard to help you to remember:
"first of all, darling – are they boys or girls?"
A silence. "I don't know. But they were lovely."

Oh, I can feel the whole thick of it shifting;
keep it light, keep it light. We hop on our little legs,
their feathery ends tapping out empty messages
One-two-three-four on top of the shuddering custard.

Urn

That was the word you wanted. Once again
you started on the story of the day
your neighbour went to scatter his Dad's ashes.
I closed my eyes, letting you drift un-chivvied
among encouraging *umms* – (yes, love, I'm listening) –
until you found your way of saying it,
a stunning fragment of pentameter.
"It's like a bottle with his body in it."

"Ah, yes," I said, not giving you the word
because your meaning had no need of it.
Instead, my right hand, almost by itself,
wrote down your lovely phrase to savour later.

"It's cup-of-tea time." Ritual unhooking
with "Bye-bye darling. Love you. Speak tomorrow."
And in the satisfied purr of the hang-up
I heard the echo of another voice.

I saw with my own eyes the shrunken Sibyl
suspended in a jar, and when they asked
what she most wished for, she replied "to die".

SHE FORGETS TO PHONE

You haven't rung today, but there's still time
for "not" to turn itself into "not yet".
I've made myself another cup of tea.
This is the third day since your last phonecall.
If you don't ring me up tomorrow morning
I'll have to call to find out how you are.
Now my eyes flick from phone to clock and back.
Will it be you today or me tomorrow?

It's too late now, you will not ring today.
I rise, push back my chair and get my coat,
let myself out and head down to the shop
wondering if you're ringing while I'm gone.
That's how it is, my darling. I'm in thrall
not just to you but to my own promise
and any future freedom lies in your
eventual perpetual forgetting.

WHEN I HAVE FEARS…

When Keats had fears that he might "cease to be"
before he'd written all his mind could hold,
he recognised that his infirmity
might rob him of the chance of growing old.
The lucky youngster never lived to see
coevals gradually lose their grip
on memory, on personality
and the last precious dregs of scholarship.
He never got to watch the tragedy
of shared affairs no longer making sense
between good friends, nor feel the absentee
tottering into total nescience,
so he could not have understood that what
I'm most afraid of is that I might not.

SOLSTICE

The top is spinning slower, the sound changes.
It lurches on the last part of its story
and those who know this are already grieving.

Raven coughs like an old man in the morning
clearing his cluttered pipes so as to curse
the need to rise for such a little day.

Buzzard flies lower, so that all can hear
his *oh, oh, oh* against a sepia sky,
his keening for the end of everything.

The young owls have grown into their voices,
left behind the strangeness of their breaking
to hurl clear cries of loss at the early moon.

Now the top teeters, soon it will stop and fall.

But only for a moment, just until
the owner steps in to prevent its ending
and set it singing on another spin.

I THINK NOT

Your gift arrived today. I will not use it.
A cup and saucer and a matching plate
In thin bone china, rung around with roses.
You say you saw it in a little shop
And thought of me and knew I had to have it.

Well, bugger off! I do not choose to sit
With a frail thimble rattling on a dish
Or raised with a gnarled hand, my ancient pinkie
Poised in a frozen curlicue of twee.

You meant well, but the overwhelming shock
Of seeing what you see when you see me
Has quite made up my mind. I will not use it.
I'll slurp the beaded bubbles from the brim
Of a cheap beaker, full of my warm self
Until it slips and clatters to the floor
From my nerveless fingers.

SPARROWFART

Slippered and gowned and newly breakfasted
I step across the threshold, make an entrance
into the spotlight of the sudden lamp
bearing a plate of crusts and crumbs, a mug
of cooling tea in one stiff morning hand.

The door clicks shut. Then the dull ivy shivers,
the leaves move and a small sound escalates
from a soft shuffle into a clatter.
Down, down from the face of the house they tumble,
all the small sparrows from their winter roost.

I've hosted nests, defended many tenants
from cats and jackdaws, seen them through the summer,
nourished them and their fledglings alongside
all their fair-weather friends who flew away
at the first whisper of the year's turning.

Come then, you loyal denizens. Here's food
to thank you for your hard work through the night.
You kept the house alive while I was sleeping,
now fill your faces and enjoy the day.
Sparrows, let's not let one another fall.

WAY TO GO…

Carriage Return

They will collect me in a horse-drawn hearse,
brought to the front door in the early morning.
I hear it coming even though the street
is strewn with straw to muffle its approach.

Silently, and without a by-your-leave,
they take me out and lay me on the bier,
leave my achievement, squashed into a lozenge
black-framed and draped, behind me on the wall.

And off we go. Black hackneys, four-in-hand,
the leaders tossing as the wheelers nod.
Black ostrich feathers on their headpieces
moving in sequence like a stripper's fans.

Nobody sees me jump ship and turn back
to steady the hand of the street urchin
who scuttles forward with a battered bucket
to claim the bounty of their sudden dung.

I show him how to set his foot just right
and shift the shovel with a single thrust
to trap the reeking goodness up against it
so as to get the beauty of it hot.